a *changed* heart
prayers and reflections

Other Books by David Haas Available from GIA Publications

A Time to Pray: For Justice and Peace • G-68

A Time to Pray: With the New Testament • G-6654

A Time to Pray: With the Old Testament • G-6722

Biblical Way of the Cross • G-6615

Give Me Jesus • G-7501

I Will Sing Forever • G-5649

The Holy Presence of God • G-7154

To Give You a Future with Hope • G-7153

To Worship in Spirit and Truth • G-6521

With Every Note I Sing • G-4392

With You by My Side, Vol. 1: The Journey of Life • G-5785

With You by My Side, Vol. 2: Confirmation • G-5786

a *changed* heart
prayers and reflections

david **haas**

Also available

Compact Disc • CD-822

Music Collection • G-7736

GIA Publications, Inc.

Chicago

A Changed Heart: Prayers and Reflections
David Haas

GIA Publications, Inc.
7404 South Mason Avenue
Chicago IL 60638
www.giamusic.com

G-7737
ISBN: 978-1-57999-797-7

To my Father,
my best and dearest friend,
for his most loving and accepting heart,
and for sharing with his son the precious gift
of hospitality, generosity,
and the love of music and life.

Contents

Introduction

At the heart of all liturgical prayer is the paschal mystery, honoring the death, life, deeds and destiny of Christ Jesus. At the liturgy we connect the big paschal story of Jesus to our story of daily dyings and risings, and respond with the discipleship that flows from the gift of our baptism. Liturgical music is a strong and concrete proclamation of this conversion journey, where we sing our belief and passion for Christ and commit ourselves to one another and the world in mission.

Our common sung prayer helps us to pray as a believing people and to sing and celebrate the presence of God. This is the journey that this most recent collection of liturgical music, *A Changed Heart*, hopes to profess.

I feel compelled to share the story that led to the creation of this music with the hope that its content and intent will be more understood as a result. Let me be clear: *A Changed Heart* is first of all a collection of music composed for the gathered assembly; but it is also a celebration of my own experience of the paschal mystery, a journey of new direction and change.

On December 6, 2007 (the Feast of St. Nicholas), I had open-heart surgery for a valve replacement and the repair of an enlarged aorta. There were several preliminary tests and procedures, including an angiogram and an MRI. The ten-hour surgery and initial days of recovery in the hospital were followed by three separate episodes of cardiac arrhythmia, leading to an additional surgical procedure to install a pacemaker/defibrillator.

After two-and-a-half weeks in the hospital, I completed a three-month program of cardiac rehab, and now, with the help of wonderful doctors and prescribed medications, I am doing very well. God is so very good, indeed!

It was an amazing experience of questioning, fear, anxiety, worry, care, love, hope, and so much more. The love, care, and prayers of family and blessed friends were—and continue to be—overwhelming for me. I am still learning so much from the entire experience, and I still seek what God is asking of me in the midst of this new chapter in my life. I have come to know God's unconditional love for us in a fresh and powerful way. In the midst of many bouts of anxiety and sadness, I know more fully that we are not alone; God and the community of faith is with us to love us, help us to survive, and move forward, even in the darkest of times.

During this period many coaxed me to share the creativity and new music they thought would naturally come from this experience. For a long time I did not feel creative at all. Creating music was not even on my screen. After time, new music eventually started to emerge, but not consciously as a response to my experience, although I can see now some of the connections.

"You Welcome in Me" is a new, prayerful reflection of Psalm 51, one of the central psalms for the season of Lent. Singing and praying this text has been recognition of God's voice speaking to me in a more pronounced way than ever before, reminding me that I am very much alive.

"Down to the River to Pray" is an arrangement of an early American folk hymn. It is a wonderful reminder that I need to pray more and that I have been blessed by so many who have held me in prayer and who continue to do so. This circle of family and friends continues to lead me to the river, helping me to remember what my baptism really means.

"You Are Always Present" is a Taizé-like mantra calling to mind the presence of God and our commitment to embody that presence with every breath. Being attentive to this closeness of God can provide courage and comfort in the most frightening and fragile times.

The wonderful canticle of Isaiah that is celebrated in "Enter God's House" has helped me confront my own demons. Being close to death has provided an opportunity to reflect on my life, my choices, and my behavior. We need to keep climbing God's mountain.

The original impetus for "We Are on Holy Ground" was a recent request to compose a song for the high school where I teach, prayerfully recognizing the sacredness of our school community. We all need to reverence and honor where we are and the wonderful saints whom we are with.

"Summer Sun or Winter Skies" is a setting of a powerful poem that Shirley Erena Murray wrote during the Christmas season that followed September 11, 2001. My surgery and the early days of recovery were during Advent and Christmastime several years later, so the juxtaposition of the Incarnation and the paschal mystery were quite real for me. Christmas comes even when there is pain and suffering, warring and loneliness, abuse and struggle. In the midst of the deepest horror, the hope of new birth is the most precious gift of Christmas.

"Alleluia: Our God Is Speaking" is an unapologetic burst of thanksgiving and praise—and there certainly has been much to give God thanks and praise for!

"Jesus Christ Is Lord" is a new setting of the moving canticle from Paul's letter to the Philippians. Accepting the cross is at the heart of discipleship. While there are many crosses to bear, we must embrace our suffering as gift as Jesus did. He is Lord of our lives, and I have certainly seen the face of Christ in those who have walked this journey with me.

What I did not expect to receive was a renewed summons to serve, which I celebrate in my musical version of Mary Louise Bringle's text, "We Will Rise Up and Follow." We face our own frailties, and we learn to be more present and attentive to the burdens of others: to live, speak, listen, and act as Jesus.

I have also learned to honor more deeply those taking the final steps of their life journey, which led to "God, Grant This Suffering Soul Release," featuring a powerful text by Adam Tice. Let us hope and pray that when we finally reach the eternal embrace of God, we will hear the words "well done."

When we survive a crisis or endure an arduous journey, we need to center ourselves in gratitude and thanks to God, remaining true to our calling: "For the Glory of God." I hope that the community of friends and family that hold us in prayer will push us back to the center of this calling when we falter.

"My Soul Waits for God" is a setting of Psalm 62, a prayer of quiet assurance. It was written in response to receiving the Sacrament of the Sick. What a most gracious gift, this sacrament! The psalm celebrates the trust and hope that comes from God alone and the loving heart of the wider community of faith that is at our side during troubled times.

We need to do more than just sing the songs; we have to live and choose justice as our response to our singing and praising. "Sing a New Song" is a celebration of our common call to worship and a reminder to do so in the spirit and truth of God's freedom.

"You Are My Friends" is dedicated to my singer friends who continually help me to keep singing in the best of times and through my darker days. As God did with Jesus, we are called by name, and the name we are given is "beloved."

In the end, as the final song of this project sings, "All Is Brought to Life" in Jesus Christ. The great liturgist, the late Fr. Robert Hovda, was once chastised for having a messiah complex. His response was, "I thought we were all supposed to have one." Through our life journeys we come to know the love of Christ in the most interesting ways. With Christ, life soars; with Christ, changed hearts are possible, enabling us to seek this messiah complex and become Christ to the world.

The songs and reflections provided here are opportunities to break open the mystery of conversion and a call for hearts to change and open to Christ. In the honored practice and tradition of lectio divina, we meditate and pray upon a scripture passage that is proclaimed or read; here the primary lectio is the music—the actual song-prayer itself. Prayerfully consider both the text and its musical treatment.

As you listen to the CD and pray along with this book you will see music and lyrics on the left page and a breaking open of the message, reflection questions and a concluding prayer on the pages that follow. Use these in private prayer, as well as in group settings intended for reflection and spiritual growth (retreats, bible study groups, adult or youth catechetical events) and formation experiences for choirs, cantors, and other ministers of music. Be open to adapting and combining these reflections with the recorded music to create new worship experiences.

I write these words on the Feast of the Epiphany of the Lord at the beginning of 2010. I quivered a bit as I read the following verse from the first reading (Isaiah 60:1–6) that begins the Liturgy of the Word for this day:

> *Then you shall see and be radiant;*
> *your heart shall thrill and rejoice...*

My heart certainly thrills and rejoices as I share these prayer-songs and the reflections that accompany them here. My prayer is that those who sing and pray this music, both in the experience of liturgy and in their own prayer life, can also discover a changed heart. I hope that all who listen, sing, pray, and reflect upon these songs, canticles, psalms, and hymns will be able to make a similar journey, with changed hearts open and responsive to the glory found in Jesus Christ.

David Haas

a *changed* heart
prayers and reflections

You Welcome in Me

Track 1

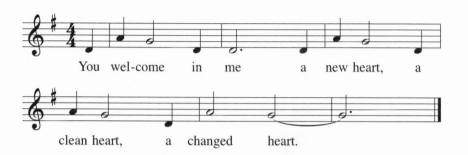

You wel-come in me a new heart, a
clean heart, a changed heart.

Have mercy, O tender God, in kindness show compassion.
Wash away my sin; free me from my shame.
I know my evil too well, my failings surround me.
Before your eyes you see me in my worst offense.

You love those who live in truth; come, fill my heart with wisdom.
Come and make me clean, wash me white like snow.
God, re-create my heart, make new in me your spirit.
Cast me not aside, keep your spirit near.

Come, bring an end to my tears, and I will sing your justice.
Give to me the words; I will sing your praise.
My gift of sacrifice will not delight or please you.
So I offer you my spirit, my changed heart you will embrace.

Text: Psalm 51; adapt. David Haas
Tune: David Haas
© 2010, GIA Publications, Inc.

To change, to really change, is a monumental calling and challenge. We all want to change ourselves in some way. We are always asking others to change as well, often for our own needs. We hear about the need for a change in direction or a change from the past. In terms of our faith and in what God is asking of us, it is not that we should change what we believe; perhaps we need to think of belief that can change us.

It is not realistic for us to expect our usual patterns of doing things to change miraculously. Completely changing our personality, or the way we communicate with people, or how we process or discern choices is difficult at best. The psalmist however, asks for a change of heart and shares with us an image of our God welcoming and embracing this new heart.

Belief that can change us is grounded soundly in our lives when that belief moves beyond intellectual assent of doctrines and theological concepts, washing over us as we truly come to know a God who loves us so lavishly and unconditionally that we are changed without even knowing it.

How does this happen? It happens when our shame is transformed by a new sense of freedom that flows from accepting our humanity as gift rather than a flaw or stain upon our existence. It comes when we experience God who lovingly but profoundly confronts all our lies and counters our creation with truth, bringing a freedom that we have never found before. It springs forth as our tears and fears are replaced with the joy and laughter of new life.

These are the things that create anew a heart that does more than beat and pulse to keep blood flowing. They help to forge a re-creation of our entire self, providing a fresh lens through which to see the world, how we treat one another, and most intimately, how we treat and care for ourselves.

God eagerly waits to make us clean, to make us new, to welcome us. But even though God has already changed our hearts over and over again, God will not act until we welcome God as our willingness to change meshes with God's strength to do so.

God does not give up on us. Kindness, compassion, and God's justice are celebrated in this psalm. We need to remember that these things are not things that God has to work at; they are intrinsic to whom God is. But for us, kindness and compassion and the passion for justice is often difficult for us to show others or to receive ourselves. Kindness, compassion, and justice are the things of God.

True belief that leads to a changed heart boldly recognizes that we do not always welcome this new heart; but God never stops waiting patiently for us to receive a most unconditional and welcoming spirit to bring about true change.

- Why do we find it difficult to welcome, as God desires for us, a new and changed heart?
- What helps us in our growth?
- How can we make kindness, compassion, and the thirst for justice real in our lives?
- What are the ways in which we can be more open to receive God's welcoming presence?

Gracious and awesome God,
you are relentless with us, always welcoming,
always kind and compassionate,
always confident that we will turn our lives around
and change our hearts.
Do not be discouraged by our failures,
but stay true to your belief
in the best parts of ourselves:
that we can and will change,
that we can and will embrace the ways
of your most compassionate heart
and join that heart in a life of joy and promise
that you want for us.

Amen.

Down to the River to Pray

Track 2

1.–5. As I went down to the riv-er to pray, stud-y-ing a-

bout that good old way, and who shall wear the star-ry

crown, good Lord, show me the way.

1. O broth-ers, let's go down, let's go down,
2. O sis-ters let's go down, let's go down,
3. O fa-thers, let's go down, let's go down,
4. O moth-ers, let's go down, let's go down,
5. O pil-grims, let's go down, let's go down,

come on down. O broth-ers, let's go down,
come on down. O sis-ters, let's go down,
come on down. O fa-thers, let's go down,
come on down. O moth-ers, let's go down,
come on down. O pil-grims, let's go down,

1.–5. down to the riv-er to pray.

Text: American folk hymn; adapt. David Haas

Tune: American folk hymn; arr. David Haas

One of the many countercultural aspects of the Christian life is our clinging to each other in community. Alongside our passionate belief in the Real Presence in the consecrated bread and wine of the Eucharist is our equally passionate stance that Christ is present in each of us in the gathered assembly, the human community of believers, the Body of Christ.

We are all together on the Christian journey: brothers, sisters, fathers, mothers, pilgrims all—all one family, called to form ourselves in the faith ("studyin' about that good old way"), to hold each other up ("show me the way"), and to live in an ongoing and lifelong relationship with Christ in response to our baptismal call ("let's go down to the river to pray"). While it is certainly fine to witness about our personal relationship with Jesus, it does violence to such a graced relationship to ignore each other, to not recognize and celebrate the presence of the Holy in the wonderful tribe of believers.

This wonderful old folk hymn centers us in the basic firmament of our faith: we need to make a daily and passionate choice for Christ; we need each other; and we need to pray. Without the grace of such ongoing practices—if we stop going down to the river to re-ignite our mission—our choice for Christ becomes weary, tired, ordinary, and dull. We eventually burn out.

Nothing can replace the power and strength that prayer provides. So, when we feel anxious, let us pray. When we feel grateful and hopeful, let us pray. When we feel discouraged, let us pray. When we feel alone, let us pray. When we seem to be out of focus, let us pray. When those around us are hurting, let us pray. When things seem overwhelming and hopeless, let us pray. When we feel so full of gratitude we think we will burst wide open, let us pray. In all things, let us keep going down to the river to pray.

- What happens to us when we feel we are drowning in our ache to pray?
- How is the image of the river like a refreshing place to build up community?
- Where do we find the kind of community that keeps us moving forward in faith?

Gracious and awesome God,
we continually come to know you more deeply
in the presence of each other.
Come now
and give us the energy to keep moving
toward the river of life
which keeps us strong in our faith
and connected to you.
Come now
and make us into one family:
sisters, brothers, mothers, fathers,
pilgrims on the journey
to your river,
to your presence,
to your loving embrace.

Amen.

You Are Always Present

Track 3

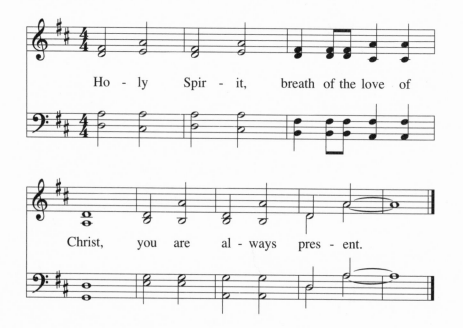

Ho - ly Spir - it, breath of the love of Christ, you are al - ways pres - ent.

Call us now to be your love, always present.
Call us now to be your hope, always present.
Call us now to be your light, always present.
Call us now to be your peace, always present.
Call us now to be your word, always present.
Call us now to be your hands, always present.
Call us now to be your eyes, always present.
Call us now to be your heart, always present.

Text: David Haas
Tune: David Haas

We always seem to be looking for God. The search to be in God's presence and to feel the Spirit moving in us, to come to know Christ in a personal and intimate way, seems to be a primary ache for Christians, especially in prayer. Many of us expect to feel something extraordinary or paranormal when we experience the presence of God. We often feel that if we can somehow grasp and attain this kind of unworldly experience we will find peace, and at that moment discover what the Risen Christ is asking of us.

At the start we need to unlearn some of our own presumptions about how and where we find God. The Risen Lord is always present through the power of the Holy Spirit. Christ is not hidden, although we ourselves often want to hide. Christ is not far away, although we are sometimes encouraged to feel that we have to make long-distance pilgrimages to discover a glimpse of the transcendent. Yes, Christ is certainly present in the elements of consecrated bread and wine. Yet we sometimes genuflect before the tabernacle while simultaneously ignoring—and sometimes even profaning—the presence of Christ in the community of baptized believers.

Christ is not far away. Christ is here. Now. Always. The Spirit is truly the "breath of the love of Christ." This precious breath is all around us: in creation, and in the wonderfully blessed and broken humanity of our brothers and sisters: those we love, and those whom we find it difficult to love. We are, in a way, called to be a second coming of Christ, the ongoing breath of the love of Christ. If we are present, then Christ is present. But that presence is not something to hoard in isolation.

To recognize and celebrate this presence is an obligation to further and deepen that presence. If we say "yes" to Christ, we must say "yes" to the call to love, to be a message of hope, to lighten a darkened world, to be peacemakers; to be the hands, eyes, and heart of this presence. It cannot stay stagnant. It must move. This presence must explode from everything we say and do. This eternal and endless presence cannot remain hidden or absent. It is a call, and we are called to be a living and relentless proclamation of its message.

- What makes it difficult for us to recognize Christ's presence? What helps us to overcome these difficulties?
- Who are the people who most mediate that presence in our lives?
- How can we be more attuned to Christ's presence in all people, times, and places?

Gracious and awesome God,
you are here.
Come and pull away all things
that keep us far from you.
Come and instill in us a deeper awareness
of how and where we can discover you:
in the most majestic and dramatic of things,
and in the most ordinary and simple of things.
Call us to be awake,
to see you, to feel you,
and to proclaim you
with the entirety of our lives—
to love lavishly,
to hope faithfully,
to enlighten joyfully,
to bring peace passionately;
to be your hands, eyes, and heart to all—
always,
without hesitation
and without distinction.

Amen.

Enter God's House

Track 4

All you na - tions, all who seek peace:

leave your arms and weap-ons be - hind.

Come and climb the moun-tain of God.

En - ter God's house!

In the final times, the temple will rise above the highest point.
In the final times, all nations will move upon it,
and all will say, "Let us climb God's mountain to see Jacob's house,
and we will learn the way and path of truth."

And our God will end the wars that divide, and calm the conflicts of all.
And the swords will turn to plows and spears to pruning hooks.
And the nations will destroy their weapons and train no more for war.
House of Jacob, come and walk in the light of God!

Text: Isaiah 2:2–5; adapt. David Haas
Tune: David Haas
© 2010, GIA Publications, Inc.

The vision of Isaiah in this canticle may seem naïve or utopian, and not realistic at all. It may seem at first glance to be an overly simplistic solution to the eternal, inevitable, and timeless evil of war, violence, and genocide. Isaiah seems to simply say, "Stop your war making; put down your weapons; be above these things, seek God's vision of a reign where such behavior is not necessary at all. Just embrace God's way: seek peace, stop the warring!" This approach seems death-dealing for most of us; it is too risky, too hard, and makes everyone too vulnerable. One cannot negotiate this way, as the other side cannot be trusted.

Common wisdom is that peace can only be achieved through strength and possibly threatening harm toward those whom we perceive to be our enemy. Such attitudes flourish not only in the warring of nations, the issues of world security, and global politics. We transfer these principles and attitudes to others in our daily relationships with them in the most ordinary circumstances of human existence.

We cannot possibly let our guard down in our relational conflicts; we have to have the upper hand, we have to have some source of power, a weapon that will help us prevail and conquer the other. It is the human response. It is just too naïve and too hard to simply "put our weapons down" and climb the mountain where an alternative way may be waiting for us. We find it impossible to wrap our minds around the possibility that the task of peace certainly can be attained in what seems to be such a passive approach.

But, ah! It is that simple, it is that uncomplicated. This human response is not God's response to our violent and warring world. And yes, quite simply, we are called to change—change our way, change our strategy—because if we are honest, we know that the present way of doing things is not working. Perhaps it works temporarily in some cases, creating some sort of short-term peace that is based in fear, not in love and the reverencing of the most precious gift of human life.

This so-called peace is really not peace at all, the true shalom that is central to the Jewish tradition. With short-term peace based in fear, the pressure cooker is always turned up high, and the weapons and tools for war are certainly not transformed into pruning hooks.

It is simple. We need to intentionally, simply, leave our arms and weapons behind. If we are lovers of the Word and believe in God, there is really no other way to read or manipulate these words.

Why are we so afraid? We are asked to leave behind the anger and rage that leads to destruction, violence, abuse, and horror. Let us climb the mountain of God and discover the path of love and justice, not only for the sake of world tensions, peace, and politically safe foreign policy, but so that, in the quiet of our hearts, God may lead us to healing, reconciliation, and the dance of delight in all humanity, in all creation.

- What deeply embedded fears lead us to war-like behavior and hatred?
- Where is that fear in us?
- Who are the models and witnesses around us that are in sync with Isaiah's vision?
- How can we find the courage to embrace and live God's peace?

Gracious and awesome God,
we ache for your guidance and strength
to heed the words and attitudes of peace,
your true shalom, a peace that the world cannot give,
but a peace that the world truly needs.
Come now, and instill in us the fervor and passion
that can lead us to choose a new way,
that can lead all of us
to a more true and lasting peace;
a peace that produces growth and nurture,
not violence and senseless abuse of life.
Show us your peace, a peace that is truly so.

Amen.

We Are on Holy Ground

Track 5

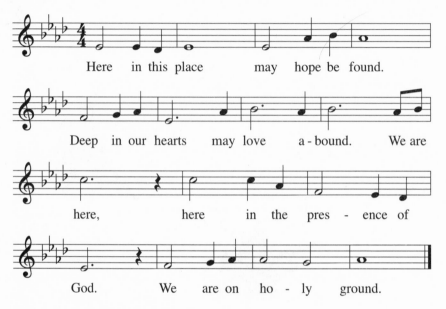

Here in this place may hope be found.

Deep in our hearts may love a - bound. We are

here, here in the pres - ence of

God. We are on ho - ly ground.

May your presence make us pause;
may your vision be our cause.
May the gifts that we enjoy
find a way to sing your joy.

May your calling be the way;
may we always teach and pray.
May the ones now in our care
be the center of our prayer.

May we seek a wider view;
may our faith in you be true.
May the passion we impart
fill each young and hungry heart.

Text: David Haas
Tune: David Haas
© 2010, GIA Publications, Inc.

Our baptism is a call to serve, to teach, to evangelize. But if our service begins and ends with seeing this baptismal life as merely surrendering to doctrines and precepts, it fails. To teach is to witness to the way of Christ to the best of our ability. How did Jesus primarily do this? The center of his "catechetical method" was his passionate love and honor of his people, unequaled hospitality, reverence for the poor, and a loving heart. All in his presence were changed and affected in profound ways.

We are called to continue Jesus' way of prophetic proclamation of God's presence and activity in our lives. Yes, we are charged with being the presence of Christ to all, bound together with an attentiveness to recognize that most holy presence in all those we serve; to recognize that wherever we are, and wherever God's people are, it is holy ground.

Our gifts are that: gifts shared to help reveal God's passionate care. Our teaching is to be transparent, meaning that our words must be the very words of God; our eyes to reveal how God sees everyone, and our hands to serve as God desires.

Our prayer life is fully realized when it is a spiritual conversation with God in which we lift the concerns and care of those we teach and catechize. We are asked to always broaden our sight to see through the lens of God's promise, and to be passionately attentive and present to all who hunger for God in their lives, regardless of their age, their station, their biases, and the diversity of their expressions and beliefs.

A line from Les Misérables provides a wonderful guide: "to love another person is to see the face of God." This is the ministry of teaching, to be a catechist, one who echoes the Word. We cannot recognize that the face of God is truly present in each other until we first recognize the holy ground in which we all dwell and make the journey of life.

Whenever we are attentive and present to God's people, whenever we share and experience each other's stories of faith, whenever our dyings and risings are experienced and celebrated, it is a holy encounter. We are on holy ground.

- What are the ways in which we honor the many different people we encounter?
- How can we refocus our attitudes to free ourselves to see the face of Christ in each other?

- The places where we live, work, and worship—are they holy ground for us? If not, why not?

Gracious and awesome God,
help us to see every encounter,
every place where we walk,
every life we intersect,
as a dwelling of your holy presence.
Open our eyes to see your activity in every life,
open our ears to hear your voice in every utterance,
open our minds to be filled with the wisdom
that lies in every child of God,
open our hearts to receive the loving compassion
that you have instilled in all humanity,
and open our hands to embrace and recognize
your movement in all things.
We know and believe that we walk on holy ground.
Come and guide our steps on the journey.

Amen.

Summer Sun or Winter Skies

Track 6

1. Sum - mer sun or win - ter skies, Christ-mas comes— shep-herds, an - gels, lull - a - bies, words re - cord-ed by the wise: read it in the book— take an - oth - er look. . . .

2. Shad - ows track the hawk in flight Christ-mas now— chil - dren born in fire and fight, si - lent night a vio-lent night, hawks are in con - trol of a na - tion's soul

3. There where ter - ror plies its trade Christ-mas now— chil - dren learn to be a - fraid, mine-fields of dis-trust are laid, e - vil is in force on a win - ning course

4. Child of peace, God's hu-man face, Christ-mas now— come to plead war's coun-ter-case, bring the dove a nest-ing place, though her wings are torn, though her blood is drawn

5. Win - ter skies or sum-mer sun Christ-mas comes— still the threads of hope are spun, good - ness will out-class the gun, e - vil has no tooth that can kill the truth.

Text: Shirley Erena Murray,

© 2003, Hope Publishing Company, Carol Stream, IL 60188.

All rights reserved. Used by permission.

Tune: David Haas, © 2010, GIA Publications, Inc.

This contemporary carol confronts us with an obvious counterpoint to the typical proclamation of the mystery of Christmas.

We have so many assumptions about the Incarnation and the many rituals, attitudes, and values that this season presents. One is the "winter-only" way in which Christmas is seen, both in terms of weather and mood. The author of this text lives in New Zealand, where Christmas is celebrated in the heat of summer. Another assumption is the naïve and immature way in which we often read, pray, and live the birth narratives and the myths and nostalgia they unfortunately breed.

This season often embraces a sentimental piety that ignores the realities of our world, leading to an isolation of the human, political, and religious dynamics that are in direct conflict with the message of the Incarnation.

Lurking in and around the messages of joy, gladness, and cheer that this season should indeed celebrate is the reality of loneliness and war, violence and genocide, greed and selfishness, racism and deep sadness.

We have been taught that the season of Advent celebrates two comings: the historical incarnation of Jesus Christ born into our history, and the advent of God in the final times, the in-breaking of the Reign of God. But there is a third coming that we tend to forget. We also call to mind the coming of Christ into our own existence, right here, right now, in our time. And what is the state of the world in which our beloved Christ enters and is made known?

This carol reveals a broken, war-torn, and violent world. The text was written soon after the events of September 11 2001, and graphically presents the world in which Christmas comes. It pokes holes in the sentimental attitudes that accompany our understandings and somewhat shallow beliefs about Christmas. Christmas is not about the birth of the Baby Jesus alone: it is about new life and hope in the midst of a hopeless situation, where life is often abused; it is about the Prince of Peace coming into a world where peace is mocked; it is about a promise made in a time when promises are shabby and empty. Ultimately, it is about Love born into a frenzy of hatred and fear. But ultimately, it is about a Christ whose power can and will truly "outclass the gun."

Christmas is about the truth—the truth of how things really are, and our faith in our greatest and most treasured truth: Jesus, the Christ, born into the center of our stories and providing hope for our destiny.

- What is it about this time that often numbs us from seeing the truth?
- How can we move forward and become more authentic bearers of the message of Christmas?
- How do our lives portray "Christmas comes" this year?

Gracious and awesome God,
in the midst of all that the world is and will be, you come.
In the midst of all that is evil and horrific, you come.
In the midst of our hopelessness and despair, you come.
Come now, and remove our blindness,
to see clearly how things really are in our world,
in our relationships,
and in our own hearts.
Come now, and fill us with the hope
that comes from you alone,
and the truth that will truly
bring your presence to birth.

Amen.

Alleluia: Our God Is Speaking

Track 7

Refrain

Al-le-lu-ia, al - le - lu - ia! Al-le-lu-ia, al - le - lu - ia! Al-le-lu-ia, al - le - lu - ia! Al - le - lu - ia, al - le - lu - ia! Al - le - lu - ia, al - le - lu - ia!

Verse Responses

Al - le - lu - ia, al - le - lu - ia! Al-le-lu-ia, al - le - lu - ia!

Our God is speaking, bold and clear.
Spirit of Jesus, now be here.

Our God is moving, sure and strong.
Spirit of Jesus, be our song.

Our God is stirring, we rejoice.
Spirit of Jesus, be our voice.

Text: David Haas
Tune: David Haas
© 2010, GIA Publications, Inc.

"Alleluia!" For believers, it is our most prized, precious, and common acclamation and utterance of praise, sung and shouted throughout the ages. Its meaning is "Praise the Lord!"

The center of all worship and liturgical life is the offering of praise. But this praise is always a response to God's activity, God's presence, God's speaking and breaking through the silence and isolating sadness of our human existence. With the exception of Psalm 150 (which is an unapologetic litany of praise), all of the praise psalms found in the Psalter express praise in answer to or as a result of the movement of God in the midst of loneliness and despair, questioning and doubt, or tumult of some kind. Praise is almost never absent following a situation of suffering or sadness.

God speaks and moves, acts and stirs, dances and sings in the midst of our lonely songs of journey and anxiety. God speaks, penetrating the deafness of a world self-consumed. God moves in a world that often chooses to stand still. God stirs things up when we become too complacent or predictable. Though we may choose to cover our ears, though we may close our eyes, though we may attempt to shut down the compassion of our hearts, God is relentless in toppling our opposition. God is here, very active, moving, stirring, and always speaking!

May we always find a way to rejoice, shout praise, and sing "Alleluia!"

- What are the things in our lives that give us reason to shout praise?
- How has God spoken in our lives during times when all seemed hopeless?
- How are we invited to stay open to God speaking in our lives?

Gracious and awesome God,
you alone are worthy of our praise!
When we have been blind, you have opened
our eyes!
When we have been deaf to your love, you
have spoken loudly and clearly!
When we have closed our hearts to your
compassion,
you have embraced us with mercy and love!
When we have neglected to reach out in
service to others,
you have stirred our will to be your
disciples.

Come now,
and keep us faithful to your wonderful
ways.
Come now,
and keep us singing for joy.
Come now,
and keep the "Alleluias" coming forth from
our lips,
our hearts,
and with the entirety of our lives.

Amen.

Jesus Christ Is Lord

Track 8

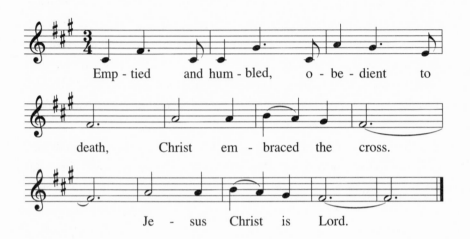

Emp - tied and hum - bled, o - be - dient to death, Christ em - braced the cross.
Je - sus Christ is Lord.

Although he was in the form of God,
he did not claim equality with God
as something to be grasped.
But Jesus chose to empty himself,
and take the form of a slave,
human and broken like one of us,
human and broken like one of us.

Being found in human form,
flesh and blood like each of us,
Jesus humbled himself.
He embraced his death, death on a cross,
and yet our God did lift him high,
with a name above all names,
with a name above all names.

So at the name of Jesus,
all knees on earth will humbly bend,
in heaven, earth, and all below,
and with one tongue proclaim and sing
all glory to our creator God:
"Jesus Christ Lord!
Jesus Christ is Lord!"

Text: Philippians 2:6–11; adapt. David Haas
Tune: David Haas

Once again we have a powerful and compelling picture of how Jesus confronts and destroys all assumptions and widely held beliefs of what it means to have power, and how that power should be used. In this New Testament canticle we see an important and prophetic summary of Paul's theology of power and how Jesus shakes up the usual models of leadership.

Jesus does everything but grasp or manipulate power. Rather, he empties himself and surrenders the trappings that most seek. Jesus' power is transformative, seeking the most unusual path of reducing oneself to slave status and freely choosing to be emptied of all the seductions associated with domination. Here is where God's glory is most celebrated and honored; here is where discipleship is discovered; here is where followers of Jesus look for strength and focus.

The seductions that Jesus rejects are all around us, regardless of our vocational choices. They are with us in our places of employment, in our relationships, and yes, even in our ministry in the church. The lure of choices that lead to power is sometimes obvious, sometimes subtle and hidden. Leadership is a tricky thing, and the qualities of humility, self-sacrifice and other-centeredness do not seem intrinsic to the seminars, books, and other training materials that guide us to become leaders.

Paul's canticle presents a Jesus who utterly fails at achieving power and influence as the world presents it. But Jesus was not interested in that kind of success. Jesus was about something so different, something so radically against the agreed-upon values and belief systems of leadership and power.

The same was true for the early Christian community. Proclaiming "Jesus Christ is Lord" was a major affront to the state. It signaled turning from allegiance and honor to Caesar to giving these to God. It was an act of treason. These four words, "Jesus Christ is Lord," made up the earliest creed, the most fundamental profession of faith for those who risked everything to be followers of the Way— namely, the way of Jesus. For them, following Christ required the surrender of all things the world finds attractive, all things that their culture—and ours—values and rewards with high honors.

The simple truth is that following Jesus, being a Christian, is hard. It means more than tolerating or accepting being humbled and emptied of self. It's more than giving assent to the struggles and sacrifices that come with discipleship. It means embracing the life of surrender, freely choosing and rejoicing in obedience to the way of Christ. It means seeing the reality and cost of humility and emptiness as a most precious gift.

- What seductions in our lives keep us from Christ-centered leadership?
- What new commitments do we need to make so that Jesus Christ will be Lord of our lives in a new and energized way?
- Who are the saints, heroes, and living witnesses who inspire us to live as disciples?

Gracious and awesome God,
we offer our prayer to you
with full acceptance of our weaknesses,
and our compliance and assent to all those things
which keep us from your path,
your values,
and your vision for how we are to live.
Come and give us the strength
to surrender,
to empty ourselves,
to embrace the humble way of your Son,
Jesus, the Christ: our way, our path, and our Lord.

Amen.

We Will Rise Up and Follow

Track 9

We will rise up, rise up and fol-low,

Christ be - fore and be - side us,

Lov - ing Pat-tern to guide us,

as we an - swer the call.

From the nets of our labors, through the noise and confusion;
from the city or seashore, Jesus summons us all.
When we faint and grow weary from the bearing of burdens,
with a message of comfort, Jesus summons us all.

In the eyes of the stranger—tearful, joyous, or frightened—
in the face of each neighbor, Jesus summons us all.
When we hear words of hatred spreading fear and false witness,
words that cry to be challenged, Jesus summons us all.

In each moment of courage, steadfast even through trembling,
in the yearning for justice, Jesus summons us all.
Like disciples before us, from the city or seashore,
risking selves in compassion: Jesus summons us all.

Text: Mary Louise Bringle, © 2006, GIA Publications, Inc.
Tune: David Haas, © 2010, GIA Publications, Inc.

There is a bumper sticker that reads, "Speak the truth, even when your voice shakes."

Christian vocation is more than specific career choices, or even the private choices of morality and lifestyle. Following Christ means rising up and rejecting a passive or gentle assent to belief expressed in doctrines alone. It is a call to surrender our very selves to patterns and choices that go against the general assumptions of a more devotionally centered faith. It is answering the ultimate call to live, love, act, and speak in the most uncomfortable or secure circumstances, and speaking truth, justice, and compassion, especially when the risk is high.

The call is for all of us, regardless of our age, race, gender, or status. All that matters is our baptism, and that God has called us to live fully and with intention. We must see our vocation as real, not just during the working hours of ministry but in every living and breathing moment and encounter: "in the eyes of the stranger… in the face of each neighbor…when we hear words of hatred…." It is a summons for sure, a summons to muster our courage, our love, and our commitment, "like disciples before us…risking selves in compassion."

In the world of the practical it is an invitation to answer hatred with love, to respond to fear with hope, to counter lies with truth, to fight the finality of death with the beauty and promise of new life. This stance and witness is not just to be embraced in the major dramatic choices that come to us occasionally in specific times of transition. The choices and call to live with the integrity of the way of Christ requires us to wake up and accept these values every day. We must accept them in the ordinary and non-romantic moments of our human struggle and in the small things that lead to profound evil. We must accept them in the subtle instances of life that more truthfully test our character and our identity as followers of the risen Jesus.

Our vocation, our call, is far more than just being nice. Gospel living demands and expects us to rise up, to follow with total loyalty and surrender, and to trust the loving pattern of Christ to guide us in every thing we do, in everything we say, in every act of living that we have as long as we have breath.

- What kind of vocational commitment are we called to make as Christians?
- Who and what are the sources of support that can help us rise up and follow Christ more faithfully?
- What are some of the specific choices we need to make, large and small, to be more true to our commitment to follow and serve Jesus?

Gracious and awesome God,
we know and believe
that you call each and everyone of us by name
to rise up and follow you
with all that we have, all that we are,
and with all that we long to become.
Instill in us a new and unwavering strength
to make choices big and small
that place you before and beside us.
Enliven in us the courage
to answer hatred with love,
fear with hope,
and evil with justice.
Help us, guide us
as we answer your call
each and every day.

Amen.

God, Grant This Suffering Soul Release

Track 1

1. God, give your faith-ful ser - vant peace; you
2. In - to your o - pen hands re - ceive this
3. God, help us all com-plete this race, to

have in-spired the fi - nal breath. You grant the
spir - it, for the bod - y dies. Grant us the
live so when our course is run, when we at

suf - f'ring soul re - lease, free from earth's
grace to ful - ly grieve as we now
last reach your em - brace, we too will

pain in time - ly death.
loose our for - mer ties.
hear you say, "Well done."

Text: Adam M. L. Tice, © 2009 GIA Publications, Inc.

Tune: David Haas, © 2010, GIA Publications, Inc.

If we are truly honest, even those of us with the strongest and most inspiring faith in the paschal mystery and the final glory of eternal life with God still find the acceptance of death painfully difficult. Whether it is a tragic and horrific cause such as an accident or terminal disease, or the most natural process of old age, the death of one close to us is a hard reality to accept. It is painful, pure and simple. We long for more time with the one who has died; we do not want to detach our ties. We just do not want them to go away, to be far from us, to be absent from our lives.

Watching and making the journey with one who is dying is two-fold: it is not just their passing, but also our own passing into a new reality. Now things are different, and will continue to be different than they were before. The experience of walking with the dying also confronts us with our own vulnerability, our own humanity, and our own future fate. Almost nothing in life is assured except for the fact that every single one of us will die one day. There is no escape. It is going to happen.

But for those of us who embrace the risen Christ, there is a most profound and powerful gift that accompanies us on this journey. We hold tightly to the belief that in death there is a greater reality, a movement that frees us from the earth's pain to experience the open hands of a God who loves us so unbelievably. This God offers release from all that is painfully human, all that has been a source of excruciating suffering, and provides the precious safe haven of peace.

When we gather at the bedside of the dying and when we share the stories at a wake; when we gather around the table to dine with the Risen Lord in the midst of a grieving community; and when we throw remnants of the earth upon the casket at burial—ultimately, these rituals and movements are at the heart of why we believe in God. These moments that both test us and strengthen us, as well as our supportive family and friends who help us to survive the pain of it all, reveal the face of God. The ironic blend of the horror and sadness of grief with the rejoicing found in the release of suffering help us invest in the notion of paschal mystery beyond doctrinal platitudes. It makes dying and rising real—and a most glorious gift at that!

- Who do we know right here, right now, in the midst of this journey?
- How can we make our rituals of dying and passing become moments of grace?
- What image or memory of someone dying well can help prepare us for our final death?

Gracious and awesome God,
we are your servants,
the living face of your presence.
Grant us the grace to fully grieve
when we face the loss of those in our lives
who have been your presence to us.
Help us to let go and rejoice
in the glorious promise of life and death,
all pointing to the most glorious gift
that you give each and every one of us:
the moment when we see you
face to face.

Amen.

For the Glory of God

Track 11

Responses

1. True to our call - ing!

2. For the reign of God!

3. All for the glo - ry of God!

We are the salt of the earth: True to our
    calling!
We are the salt of the earth: For the reign of
    God!
Where compassion is found,
the broken find a home and are made
    whole:
All for the glory of God!

We are the light of the world: True to our
    calling!
We are the light of the world: For the reign
    of God!
Where the blind now will see,
the lost will find a lamp to guide their way:
All for the glory of God!

We are new hope for the poor: True to our
    calling!
We are new hope for the poor: For the reign
    of God!

Where the hungry are fed,
the lame can walk, the lowly now find joy:
All for the glory of God!

We are the Body of Christ: True to our
    calling!
We are the Body of Christ: For the reign of
    God!
Where all people are one,
in Jesus Christ, our brother and our Lord:
All for the glory of God!

We are the People of God: True to our
    calling!
We are the People of God: For the reign of
    God!
Where good news is heard,
the way of peace and justice is our song:
All for the glory of God!

Text: David Haas • Tune: David Haas
© 2010, GIA Publications, Inc.

I live in wintery, snowy Minnesota. The winters can be rough, and when freezing rain comes and blends with snow, the roads can be, suffice it to say, very treacherous and extremely dangerous. Driving becomes a very risky venture. But then trucks come and lay salt on the surface. When the salt is well laid and of good quality, the car grips the road with confidence. I am more peaceful knowing that the salt is on the ground before I go out to drive.

I am also one who does not like darkness. When I am in a dark room, I have an urgent need to turn on the lights, sometimes to the consternation of others in the room. Even when I sleep I like having at least a night-light. It helps me feel safe.

Salt for the earth, light for the world—these are images of God that we are called to embody. As salt helps a car stay steady on the road, we are asked to be that same steadiness, that same grounding force for those negotiating their way on the path of life. As light in the darkness helps us all to see and to feel more joyful and positive, we too are asked to shine in the lives of those who seem to only know a dim and darkening life. We are called to provide beacons for them as they map their way to a better destination.

When we embrace the qualities and callings of being salt and light, we plow and lighten a path for security, peace, wholeness, and hope. When we do so, we can say with faith and confidence that we truly are the Body of Christ for one another. When we do so, our identity as people of God rings true.

Our vocation and calling is active involvement in mission, not to sit back and watch. Our witness is to be one of compassion, feeding the hungry, comforting the sightless, helping the challenged find their steps, bringing community to the lonely, and where Good News is not just a subtitle for the written New Testament, but something real, felt, and known by those who ache for hope. We are on mission for the glory of God. We do this not alone, but in solidarity with one another, the people of God, true to our calling. If we serve one another, we serve God, for that is where God is. God is in our service.

- In what situations are we called to be salt and light?
- Who are the role models and mentors inspiring us to be true to our calling?
- What kind of new commitment can we make as disciples on mission?

Gracious and awesome God,
you call us all to share in your most important mission:
to be salt, light, and hope for all.
Awaken our true calling
and deepen our resolve
to serve the least of our sisters and brothers
in their path of struggle and pain.
May we always keep your vision alive,
so that in everything we do,
we will follow our true calling
to sing, dance,
and proclaim your justice, your compassion,
and your glory.

Amen.

My Soul Waits for God

Track 12

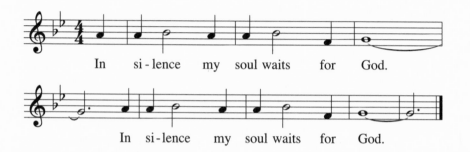

In si-lence my soul waits for God.

In si-lence my soul waits for God.

In God alone I will survive:
my rock, I stand unshaken;
my haven,
I shall not be moved.

In God I find my completion,
my strength and my direction,
protection;
my trust is in God.

In God is my mountain of hope,
my faith, my strength, my story,
my glory,
my breath and my life.

Text: Based on Psalm 62; David Haas
Tune: David Haas

The psalms are such powerful prayers of faith, embracing the entire galaxy of human emotions and experiences. Psalm 62 is no exception. In this particular psalm we pray the truth that only God is worthy of our trust. In the midst of attack by our enemies, both outside and within, we have an amazing peace that no one else can provide. In the midst of all of the noise that can deafen our sanity, a tranquil voice comes. It is the voice of God. And that voice most authentically comes in prayerful silence. This is hard, because being silent, being still and quiet at the center, is a most difficult challenge. We all seek it, those of us who are extroverts as well as the more introverted.

The grace of prayer, of truly hearing and knowing the presence of God, is a gift that eludes us all most of the time. Prayer in its most basic form often becomes an exercise of asking God for something and waiting for it to happen. When our request is denied or does not find fulfillment to our liking, we are tempted to resort to believing that God did not answer our prayers. Actually, God always answers our prayers. The problem is that we do not always like the answer.

We all have our preferred ways to pray. But regardless of what form of prayer we engage in, true prayer, true connection with God, is about discernment. We desperately want to know God's plan for us. Asking for something and magically receiving an answer does not nurture discernment. Prayer is about being still, not doing all of the talking, and intentionally listening to what God is trying to say. If we can discipline our minds and our hearts to truly listen, to be still, and to wait, then we can experience God, our rock and strength, who is our survival, our direction, our protection, our hope, and our very source of breath.

- What are the struggles in our prayer life?
- Why is it so difficult to be still, to be quiet, to be open to God speaking?
- What patterns and places can we discover to help us find stillness in our lives?

Gracious and awesome God,
we desperately need to hear your voice
and to know your direction for our lives.
Come now
and grace us with the quiet needed to place us
in silence with you
so we can hear your voice clearly,
without distractions,
without the noise that can lead us
far away from you.
Be with us in the quiet
so we can hear you,
so we can follow you,
so we can receive your strength,
so we can serve you
with the purest heart,
and with your will at the center.

Amen.

Sing a New Song

Track 13

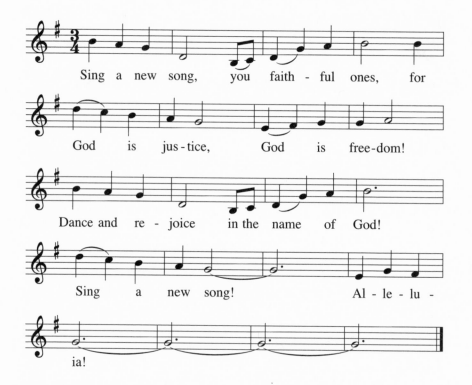

Sing a new song, you faith-ful ones, for
God is jus-tice, God is free-dom!
Dance and re-joice in the name of God!
Sing a new song! Al-le-lu-ia!

Make a new song for the people,
spin your praise everywhere!
Rejoice and dance with faith,
make music with all of your life!

Joy and delight for the people,
chosen by God with care!
With glory shout praise with your voice,
all hearts now respond with new fire!

Justice will win over evil;
oppression is now brought down!
God's reign will be our new cry;
you faithful, this is our song!

Text: David Haas
Tune: David Haas
© 2010, GIA Publications, Inc.

Somewhere, somehow, we lost the connection between good liturgy, our prayer and devotional life, and the depth of what is for many a deep secret and the essence of Catholic social teaching: our commitment to social justice. It is amazing to see so many liturgists and musicians often at odds with social justice activists and vice versa. Liturgists and musicians cite that liturgy is the source and summit of the life of the church, while the social justice folks tend to be downright anti-ritual. In their extreme, many liturgists and music ministers are concerned with creating a beautiful liturgical experience for the sake of experience, while some social justice people want political activism and change without reflection and a spiritual grounding in prayer.

Jesus proclaimed and lived this balance. He understood the necessity of blending the dynamics of right worship and justice building. And while this balance has certainly tilted back and forth throughout the history of the church, the fabric of this partnership has never been torn; it has never been insulted and separated.

We need to constantly renew this truth in our sung prayer as well as in our discipleship and work to help build the city of God. Our songs and our praise and joy in worship are authentic only when its goal and product is the work of ministry: of justice and peacemaking. Regardless of liturgical season or any other ritual action, this is the ultimate point of convergence for worship. Those of us engaged in the world and in social change need to remember that Jesus almost always had a prelude and a postlude to his miracles and actions of conversion: he took time to pray.

We need to recommit to this, to truly sing a new song, one that gathers us for prayer, gives glory to God, and provokes in us the mission given by the God of justice and freedom. It is a song about justice and goodness winning out over evil, a song that sings in the face of oppression, that calls the faithful to take on a new way—God's way.

Those of us who sing and design rituals of prayer need to find opportunities to leave the comfort of the sanctuary and discover new sacred spaces like nursing homes, hospices, prisons, and soup kitchens. Those of us who spend time lobbying at state capitols, protest events, and strategy meetings are in need of a community to pray and offer praise with, one that grounds us in the liturgy of the church. Let us be faithful. Let us dance and rejoice. Let us be people of justice and peace. Let us sing a new song.

- How do we know when our prayer life and our commitment to mission are in balance?
- How can we improve this balance in our parishes and communities of faith?
- Are we singing new songs, or the same old songs of complacency, of a tired faith?

Gracious and awesome God,
we are here as your faithful ones,
called to be living signs and songs
of your justice, of your freedom,
of your most holy and blessed name.
Be with us
and give us the voice needed
to sing, live, and become your new song:
a song of transformation,
a song of justice,
a song of your kingdom,
now and forever.

Amen.

You Are My Friends

Track 14

You be - lov - ed sons and daugh-ters,
on you, my chil - dren, my fa - vor rests.
I am with you now and al - ways.
I will love you to the end;
you are my friends.

Wandering, restless, hopeful, longing,
we reach toward you.
We long to see you, we are your children.

Seeking, asking, anxious, listening,
we reach toward you.
We long to hear you, we are your children.

Frightened, suffering, grieving, aching,
we reach toward you.
We long to know you, we are your children.

Text: David Haas
Tune: David Haas
© 2010, GIA Publications, Inc.

Saying "yes" to the call to follow Jesus and to respond to the baptismal call to ministry has always been difficult. When we reflect on those whom God has called over time, we are tempted to think God lacked the skills of good market research!

Moses had a speech impediment; Jeremiah was too young; David was too short; Jonah was hung up on fish. Job was manic-depressive; Mary was too young, and she was single; John the Baptist was too much of a hippie and downright weird (he ate bugs); Zacchaeus was too much tax-collector. Mary Magdalene and other women in Jesus' life were just that—female. Peter was constantly missing the mark—he wanted to build tents rather than walk the walk of discipleship. He went freakish when the storm became too fierce; he was squeamish when Jesus wanted to wash his feet. He had foreshadowed the audaciousness of Errol Flynn and Luke Skywalker when soldiers came to arrest Jesus; and we all know that he denied even knowing who Jesus was. Paul was an early enemy and borderline terrorist of the early Christians before his conversion. We can go on and on....

We too, have our demons, our flaws. Our résumés are filled with reasons for God not to call on us. Yet God, through the grace of Jesus the Son, continually calls us, calls us beloved and friends, and promises to never abandon us, to always walk with us, showing us favor, certainly more than we deserve.

The baptism of Jesus and his ultimate destiny and mission are one and the same; they cannot be separated and seen as competing with each other. We are called to the same. The entirety of our lives as Christians, as followers of Jesus, is ultimately a reflection of our baptism. That walk is not without struggle, and we are called as God's children to meet the struggle head on and reach out as people of hope, to be sources of solace and comfort to our sisters and brothers. To see, hear, and know our fellow travelers on the road is to see, hear and know Christ. We are God's beloved daughters and sons, and God's favor is with us, regardless of our frailties. There is nothing we can do to destroy that relationship. Our God is that faithful. When God looks at us, we are seen as friends, so wonderful, so fantastic, so beloved. Wow. We are the children of God.

- Are we able to look into the faces of others and see them as beloved?
- How can we open each other's eyes to see ourselves as God's children?
- Who in our lives see us as God sees us—as beloved and blessed?

Gracious and awesome God,
you truly are awesome
because you see us in ways that we cannot see.
You see the very best in us,
you see us as your children,
your beloved,
your friends.
Come and give us your eyes
and your heart
so we can see the same in each other:
the beauty that you see in us.

Amen.

All Is Brought to Life

Track 15

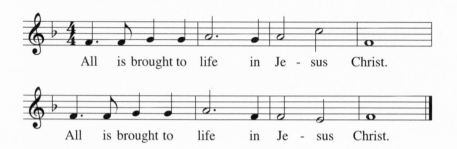

All is brought to life in Je - sus Christ.

All is brought to life in Je - sus Christ.

Christ is our hope, be glad and rejoice.

The steadfast love of God will bring rest.
By the cross of Christ, we will rise with him.

Whoever believes in Christ,
even if they die, they will live, they will live.

No one lives for oneself; no one dies for oneself.
If we live, we live for the Lord; if we die, we die for the Lord.

Christ is raised from the dead for all who are asleep.
In Christ all will live again, in Christ all will live again.

Text: 1 Corinthians 15:22, Romans 14:7–9, John 11:25–26; adapt. David Haas
Tune: David Haas
© 2010, GIA Publications, Inc.

In the musical play Fiddler on the Roof, Tevye and his friends sing a wonderful song titled "To Life." In the midst of their celebration, joy, and happiness there is a strong realization of how things are, as they sing "life has a way of confusing us, / blessing and bruising us... / God would like us to be joyful, / even when our hearts lie panting on the floor.... / and if our good fortune never comes, / here's to whatever comes." As oppressed Jews, Tevye and his community certainly know suffering, pain, and horror... and yet, in the midst of it all, they toast and sing to life!

As Christians we sometimes lose sight of the fact that our central symbol is the cross. Think about our catechumens and those who make their first step into the life of the Christian community, who begin their journey by being signed on the forehead and other parts of their body with the sign of the cross.

Let us ponder this for a moment. This ritual action is our first act of hospitality in welcoming people to become part of our community, and we do so by signing these inquirers with an instrument of death! And yet, like Tevye and his clan, these inspiring pilgrims say to us: "bring it on, because in the end, it is all about life."

All of our suffering, all of our anxieties, all of our aches and pains, all of our questions, all of our crises, all of our doubts, all of the death and destruction that we see around us—all of it, every bit of it, is eventually brought to life. Why? Because we hold our faith in Jesus Christ. His death and suffering brings sense and sanity to our sufferings and death.

Jesus did not die just for our sins. His death and his glorious rising helps us to cope, to remember that death is not the last word. It will not defeat or define us. It will not be our destiny, which is to bring all things to life. In Christ hope is not a futile or naïve feeling. In Christ the love of God is made real and human. In Christ our life and our death is a shared resurrection. In Christ we have life. In Christ we are transformed, made new, and become a living sign that says death will not win! This is our faith, and we are proud to profess it in Christ Jesus our Lord.

- What is going on in us when we feel hopeless?
- Where are the signs of transformation and life in our families, our relationships, and in the church?
- Where do we find strength to promote and empower the gift of life that God gives us?

Gracious and awesome God,
in you, in all things,
in our joys, our sufferings,
our dyings and risings,
we are made new, are brought to life.
Come now
and make us instruments of life.
Come now
and empower us to live and die for you,
to become your presence,
and your song of new life.

Amen.

Scriptural Index

Liturgical Index

Ritual Index

FUNERAL

LECTIO DIVINA

MARRIAGE

MORNING PRAYER

ORDINATION/PROFESSION/MINISTRY

PASTORAL CARE OF THE SICK

About the Music

All of the music contained in this resource is published and available as individual choral editions from GIA Publications.

CHORAL EDITIONS

All Is Brought to Life • G-7735

Alleluia: Our God Is Speaking • G-7727

Down to the River to Pray • G-7722

Enter God's House • G-7724

For the Glory of God • G-7731

God, Grant This Suffering Soul Release • G-773

Jesus Christ Is Lord • G-7728

My Soul Waits for God • G-7732

Sing a New Song • G-7733

Summer Sun or Winter Skies • G-7726

We Are on Holy Ground • G-7725

We Will Rise Up and Follow • G-7729

You Are Always Present • G-7721

You Are My Friends • G-7734

You Welcome in Me • G-7723

OTHER PRINTED AND RECORDED MUSIC COLLECTIONS BY DAVID HAAS

Title	Printed Collection	Recording
A Time to Pray: For Justice and Peace	G-6868	CD-676
A Time to Pray: With the New Testament	G-6654	CD-643
A Time to Pray: With the Old Testament	G-6722	CD-644
As Water to the Thirsty	G-3062	CD-177
Before I Was Born	G-5180	CD-448
Biblical Way of the Cross	G-6615	CD-692
Blest Are They: The Best of David Haas, Vol. 1		CD-340
Come and Journey: David Haas, Marty Haugen and Michael Joncas in Concert		CD-171
Creating God	G-3333	CD-213
Do This in Memory of Me: Holy Communion	G-5433	CD-554
Echo of Faith	G-5656	CD-507
Give Me Jesus	G-7502	CD-803
Glory Day: David Haas and Friends in Concert	G-4849	CD-390
Glory to God: The Best of David Haas, Vol. 4		CD-806
God Has Done Marvelous Things	G-4730	CD-398
God Is Here	G-6686	CD-631
I Shall See God	G-3386	CD-226
Increase Our Faith: Parish Prayer Services for Whole Community Catechesis, Year B	G-6815	CD-664
Increase Our Faith: Parish Prayer Services for Whole Community Catechesis, Year C	G-6942	CD-695
Jesus, the Compassion of God	G-4990	

Title	Printed Collection	Recording
Light and Peace: Morning Praise and Evensong	G-3079	CD-175
Living Spirit, Holy Fire, Vol. 1	G-7310	CD-716
Living Spirit, Holy Fire, Vol. 2	G-7311	CD-731
Mass for the Life of the World	G-3889	CD-285
Mass of Light	G-3341	
No Longer Strangers	G-3946	CD-298
Psalms for the Church Year, Vol. 1	G-2664	CD-167
Psalms for the Church Year, Vol. 3	G-3325	CD-212
Psalms for the Church Year, Vol. 8	G-4579	CD-387
Psalms for the Church Year, Vol. 9	G-5041	CD-430
Reach Toward Heaven	G-6151	CD-566
Singing Assembly: David Haas, Marty Haugen and Michael Joncas in Concert		CD-209
Star Child	G-5206	CD-471
Table Songs: Music for Communion, Vol. 1	G-3671	CD-265
Table Songs: Music for Communion, Vol. 2	G-6450	CD-607
Throughout All Time	G-4713	CD-392
To Be Your Bread	G-2887	CD-172
Walking by Faith	G-4831	CD-412
We Give You Thanks	G-4989	CD-436
We Have Been Told	G-2700	CD-166
When Love Is Found: Music for Weddings	G-3745	G-3745CD
Where the River Flows	G-4335	CD-349
Who Calls You By Name: Music for Christian Initiation, Vol. 1	G-3193	CD-195
Who Calls You By Name: Music for Christian Initiation, Vol. 2	G-3622	CD-257
Winter Grace: Music for Christmas and Wintertide	G-3371	CD-206
With You By My Side, Vol. 1: The Journey of Life	G-5785M	CD-517
With You By My Side, Vol. 2: Confirmation	G-5786M	CD-518
Without Seeing You: The Best of David Haas, Vol. 3		CD-805
You Are Mine: The Best of David Haas, Vol. 2		CD-341

Acknowledgments

In presenting this collection of new liturgical compositions and this book of reflections and prayers, I want to offer some thanks. I want to express my gratitude to the people at GIA Publications, especially Alec Harris, for his friendship and support, to Brian Streem, who worked very hard and offered tremendous editorial expertise and patience with the printed choral editions, and to Andrew Schultz for his artistry and talent in creating the visual design.

Thanks also to Kelly Dobbs Mickus, Tom Hawley, Michael Boschert, Ed Harris, Bob Batastini, and a special thanks to Michael Cymbala for his friendship and for being an important and integral part of my relationship and ministry with GIA over these many years.

Thanks must also be given to friends Steve Wiese and Miles Hanson at Creation Audio in Minneapolis for their creativity and hard work in engineering, mixing, and mastering the CD recording; and I also want to thank my friend Lori True for her help, ideas, and encouragement during the recording process, and also for her valued critique.

I am grateful to my mentor and friend Sr. Roberta Kolasa, SJ for her witness of ministry and service, and for providing a prayerful space at the Center for Ministry in the Diocese of Saginaw, Michigan, for me to begin writing the reflections and prayers found in these pages. Thanks also to friends Sr. Kathleen Storms, SSND, Fr. Joe Kempf, Fr. Alapaki Kim and Leisa Anslinger for their suggestions and to Gregg Sewell for his work in helping to copy edit the final manuscript.

I am continually grateful to Fr. Michael Joncas for his friendship through the many chapters of my life, and for his support and encouragement. I also am thankful for the friendship and inspiration of Bishop Remi DeRoo, Bishop Emeritus in Victoria, British Columbia, for keeping the vision and vitality of the Second Vatican Council alive.

In addition, I want to send my blessings of thanks to my singer and instrumental friends who played and sang with passion, finesse, joy and delight on the CD recording of *A Changed Heart*: Marc Anderson, Erin Anhut, Rachel Armstrong, Dave Berget, Eileen Bird, Will Creel, Lisa Cressy, Molly Dumond, Fr. Ray East, Bonnie Faber, Joel Fischer, Bobby Fisher, Jessica Garceau, Elizabeth Glover, Francis Glover, Rob Glover, Jack Gunderson, Lisa Habeck, Dick Hedlund,

Tyler Jensen, Gordy Knudtson, Steve Kron, David Livingston, Megan Mader, Freda Myhrwold, Lucia Newell, Marcia Peck, Allison Peterson, Steve Petrunak, Matt Reichert, John Snow, Zack Stachowski, Rob Strusinski, Paul Tate, Mark Thomas, Vince Therrien, Katherine True, Lori True, James Waldo, Tim Westerhaus, and Dan Westmoreland. These are the people who make the music soar, and I am grateful to them and for their tremendous talent, love and friendship.

I also want to thank Shirley Erena Murray, Mary Louise Bringle and Adam M. L. Tice for the power of their texts.

Thanks also to blessed friends and colleagues Tom Franzak, Br. Dennis Schmitz, SM, Kate Cuddy, Mary Werner, Joe Camacho, Fr. George DeCosta, Art Zannoni, Donna Peña, David Dreher, George Miller, Sr. Gertrude Foley, SC, Glenn and Kathy Baybayan, Sr. Andrea Lee, IHM, Bill Huebsch, Sr. Bridget Waldorf, SSND, Cathy Anhut, Stephen Pishner, Lynne' Gray, Alissa Hetzner, Eileen Frischmon, Patrice Pakiz, Robin Medrud, Dominic Macaller, Barbara Bridge, Dan and Jeanne Pavlina, Mary Kay Werner, Becky Gaunt, Greg Papesh, Evan Snyder, Kevin, Kim and Ken Keith, Kinohi and Akala Neves, Marty Coffman, Lisa Biedenbach, Paulette Ching, Marty Haugen, Tony Alonso, Bob Hurd, Fr. Ricky Manalo, CSP, Christopher Walker, Paul Inwood, Dr. Diana Hayes, Barbara Conley-Waldmiller, and Jo Infante.

I want to offer special thoughts of love and thanks to the amazing nurses in the 3500 wing of United Hospital in St. Paul, who were my daily life line during those most fragile days following my surgery, and to the team of doctors and surgeons who gave me (and continue to provide) such good care: Dr. William Ogden, Dr. Thomas Kersten, Dr. William Lindsay, Dr. Thomas Nobrega, and Dr. Pierce Vatterott.

Thanks also to Dr. Bob Tift, Dr. Sue Skinner, Tom Backen, Maura Brew, Holly Hoey-Germann, Becca Walsh, Joel Loecken, Mary Anderson, Dr. Sue Cipolle, May Lane, Mary Glover, Sr. Jeanne Marie Vanderlinde, OSB, Paul Keefe, and the entire Benilde-St. Margaret's High School community in St. Louis Park, Minnesota; to the entire Music Ministry Alive! family; and to Fr. Mike Byron and my parish community of St. Cecilia's in St. Paul.

Finally, I want to offer my love and thanks to my parents, and to Jeffrey, Colleen, and Helen.

About the Author

David Haas is the Director of the Emmaus Center for Music, Prayer and Ministry and serves as Campus Minister and Artist-in-Residence at Benilde-St. Margaret's High School in St. Louis Park, Minnesota.

Well known as one of the preeminent liturgical composers in the English-speaking world, he has recorded and published more than forty-five collections of original liturgical music and has written more than twenty books on the topics of music, liturgy, religious education, youth ministry, prayer, and spirituality.

He has traveled throughout the United States, Canada, the British Isles, Ireland, Europe, Australia, Israel, Greece, and Turkey as a conference and workshop speaker, concert performer, retreat leader, and recording artist, and was nominated for a Grammy Award in 1991 for the recording I Shall See God (GIA Publications).

He is a regular columnist for Ministry and Liturgy magazine and the founder and executive director for Music Ministry Alive! (www.musicministryalive.com), a national liturgical music formation program for high school and college-age youth.